PRAISE FOR *HELPING WITHOUT HURTING IN SHORT-TERM MISSIONS*

Our world is rapidly changing, even in the way we do Christ-exalting missions! In this helpful book, the Chalmers Center has given us an insightful resource that will equip short-term mission teams to avoid pitfalls of crossing cultures, especially for those embarking on communities challenged by poverty. Teams will build their capacity to learn well, honor partnerships, and maximize the good they wish to do by using this guidebook to help design their objectives with faithful presence, understanding, and humility.

John H. Sather | National Director of Cru Inner City

This [curriculum] takes the best of the revolutionary work from *When Helping Hurts* and makes it practical for short-term mission teams traveling near and far. I highly commend this resource to you as a way to serve with cultural intelligence.

David Livermore, PhD | Author of *Serving with Eyes Wide Open: Doing Short-Term Missions with Cultural Intelligence*

Being a community development organization that has sent thousands of people on short-term trips to developing countries over the years, we are thrilled to introduce Fikkert and Corbett's latest work as a relevant, vital resource for our staff and teams. It is our strong desire that every church, school, and NGO sending (or receiving) short-term teams would not only read this book, but study it—critically evaluating the work being accomplished and applying its principles to ensure teams are "helping without hurting."

Kurt Kandler | Executive Director of The 410 Bridge

If everyone responsible for sending *or* receiving a short-term service team can work through this resource—and take seriously its recommendations—I have no doubt that we will see the fruit in changed lives and stronger relationships within the global church.

Brian Howell, PhD | Professor of Anthropology at Wheaton College, author of *Short-Term Mission: An Ethnography of Christian Travel Narrative and F   ce*

Helping Without Hurting in Short-Term Missions is one of t⅃   ⅂ides on STM in print. . . . [*When Helping Hurts*] shaped t⅃   ⅂eople should think about engaging the materially r   ⅂ for short-term missioners to accompany the   ⅂n.

Daniel Rickett, PhD | Cofounder   ⅂enous
Ministries, author of *Making Your Pa*

There is no shortcut to living the inca   ⅂ in another culture. Anyone serious about truly helping wil⅃   ⅂e the value of this book and be grateful to put it to good use.

Scott Steele | Executive Director at Cherokee Gives Back Foundation

These principles will help the church move beyond good intentions and toward a discipleship model that equips team members to become lifelong missionaries wherever they are, encourages partnership with local churches globally, and truly helps advance the work of God globally.

Jeff Ward | Director of External Focus at Watermark Community Church

What really sells me on these materials is that they address what to me is the #1 question for STM participants: How do we make sure the two-week mission experience turns into a long-term commitment both to the project we visited and to serving in the communities where we live?

Kurt Ver Beek, PhD | Professor of Sociology at Calvin College

Finally, a short-term missions curriculum that gets it right! For too long church leaders have known something is wrong with the way the church does short-term missions, but not how to fix it. This book will change that. It starts with an honest appraisal of the mistakes we've been making but moves on to provide smart, practical tools to transform the way we do short-term missions. A must-read for any group that wants to do short-term missions right. Two thumbs way up!

Jo Ann Van Engen | Codirector, Semester in Honduras, Calvin College

Our short-term mission culture warrants major rethinking. This book is a priceless tool because it helps do just that, providing an alternative paradigm for cross-cultural engagement and a framework for the "messy" process of reform.

Tim Ritter | Discipleship Coordinator at Reality SF

Yes, yes, yes! This book could change the way we do missions. Every chapter is right on target, delineating the costs and complexity of a trip, and demonstrating how to make it part of long-term engagement.

Miriam Adeney, PhD | Associate Professor of Global and Urban Ministry at Seattle Pacific University, author of *Kingdom Without Borders: The Untold Story of Global Christianity*

This book challenges stewardship of our finances, encourages accountability, and acknowledges that cross-cultural interaction is an incredible process when done with plenty of grace.

McKenna Raasch | Director of Global Outreach at Calvary Church, Los Gatos

Almost no one has helped shape how our church thinks about global poverty as much as Brian Fikkert and Steve Corbett. This book furthers the discussion about effective gospel-based poverty relief strategies by translating the grand, compelling vision of *When Helping Hurts* into clear, actionable steps for churches. Our missions team has read this book, and we are implementing many of the insights within it.

J.D. Greear, PhD | author, *Gospel: Recovering the Power That Made Christianity Revolutionary* and *Breaking the Islam Code*

HELPING WITHOUT HURTING

IN SHORT-TERM MISSIONS

· · ·

Participant's Guide

STEVE CORBETT
and BRIAN FIKKERT

MOODY PUBLISHERS
CHICAGO

Crafted for the Chalmers Center by Katie Casselberry
Moody Publishers editor: Pam Pugh
Cover design: Faceout Studio
Cover image: Jacob Sjoman Svensson/Thinkstock
Interior design: Smartt Guys design

Library of Congress Cataloging-in-Publication Data
Corbett, Steve.
 Helping without hurting in short-term missions : participant's guide / Steve Corbett and Brian Fikkert.
    pages cm
 Includes bibliographical references.
 ISBN 978-0-8024-0992-8
 1. Missions--Textbooks. 2. Short-term missions--Textbooks. I. Title.
 BV2061.3.C67 2014
 266--dc23
                        2014018804

We hope you enjoy this book from Moody Publishers. Our goal is to provide high-quality, thought-provoking books and products that connect truth to your real needs and challenges. For more information on other books and products written and produced from a biblical perspective, go to www.moodypublishers.com or write to:

Moody Publishers
820 N. LaSalle Boulevard
Chicago, IL 60610

1 3 5 7 9 10 8 6 4 2

Printed in the United States of America

CONTENTS

INTRODUCTION: HOW TO USE THIS GUIDE

Over the past two decades, there has been an enormous increase in comparatively affluent churches' efforts to help the poor. One way churches are seeking to engage in poverty alleviation is through short-term missions (STMs.) After writing *When Helping Hurts*, countless church and ministry leaders approached us for further resources to design and shepherd short-term teams effectively. *Helping Without Hurting in Short-Term Missions* is designed to meet that request in a practical way.

The *Participant's Guide* you hold in your hands is the second piece of a two-part product. ***If you are a leader designing, organizing, and shepherding a short-term trip, purchase* Helping Without Hurting in Short-Term Missions: Leader's Guide. *It will guide you through the process of designing a healthy, more effective trip, which is a prerequisite to then using this* Participant's Guide *with your team.*** The material in the *Participant's Guide* will not fit well with many short-term trips as they are currently designed and practiced. It presupposes that you are taking a trip as one piece of a long-term process of learning and engagement, not as a platform for executing poverty alleviation projects. For your reference, this full *Participant's Guide* is also printed in the back of the *Leader's Guide* with additional scripting for some sections, supporting you as you lead your team through this material.

ACCESSING THE VIDEO UNITS

Units 1–5 and unit 8 are built around fifteen- to twenty-minute videos, which can be accessed by following the link or QR code printed in each unit. When prompted, set up an account with your information and the code printed in the unit. The videos are also available to RightNow Media account holders (www.rightnowmedia.org).

UNIT STRUCTURE

With the exception of unit 6, which is an on-field journaling and reflection unit, each unit will take about ninety minutes to complete. Here is a breakdown of the different sections of the lessons, as well as rough time estimates for each:

OPEN (10 minutes): This section includes preliminary questions and an introductory paragraph. Discussing the preliminary questions as a group is a vital part of mentally and spiritually preparing for the rest of the unit.

WATCH (20 minutes): Group members should close their books while watching the video so that they can fully listen to and engage with the material.

DISCUSS (40 minutes): These questions are designed to create discussion—they do not necessarily have right or wrong answers. The goal is to foster reflection, understanding, and change in participants' hearts as they consider the purpose of a short-term trip. Don't be afraid of a bit of silence; there is enormous power in having people wrestle with questions and issues together, so long as it is done in a spirit of respect.

TAKEAWAYS and **CLOSE** (10 minutes): Read this material together as you conclude the session. If your group does not have time to adequately discuss each one, contemplate the questions throughout the week.

PRAY (10 minutes): Use this final statement and prayer prompt as a call for reflection and action. Return to this prompt as you pray throughout the week.

In addition to the basic units, the resource modules at the end of this guide provide additional materials on fundraising and cultural norms.

We cannot overemphasize the centrality of prayer in this process. The principles in this guide require that all of us honestly examine our own hearts and actions as we approach STMs. Spend time praying that

God would soften your hearts as you begin the long-term process of learning and engagement with His work in the world. But also pray that your group would see, internalize, and celebrate the hope rooted in Christ.

Our brothers and sisters, both in our own communities and around the world, are proclaiming and demonstrating the good news of Christ's power and redemptive sacrifice. The journey you are about to begin is an opportunity to see, support, and move toward long-term engagement in that work. So eagerly anticipate what God will do through this opportunity, and marvel as God makes both the materially poor—and us—more of who He originally intended for us to be.

— Steve Corbett and Brian Fikkert

LEARNING AND ENGAGEMENT AGREEMENT

I, _____, recognize that by joining this learning and engagement journey, I am committing to more than simply visiting another community. I am committing to attend and participate in weeks of preparation, as well as submitting to the authority of my team leader and local hosts. Further, I am committing to stewarding the experience well, making my use of God's resources on this trip count for lasting change in my own life, attitudes, and behaviors. I agree to attend and participate in follow-up meetings with my team, where we will set concrete goals for how we might continue to support God's work of missions and poverty alleviation, encourage one another, and hold each other accountable to pursuing these goals.

Date:

Signature:

Leader's Signature:

MORE THAN
MEETS THE **EYE**

OPEN

Discuss these questions before beginning this week's unit.

• What are the first five words or phrases that come to your mind when you think of poverty?

• If you had to describe the purpose of this short-term trip in one sentence, what would it be?

• What are your personal goals for this trip? Two years from now, what are two things in your life and actions that you would like to be different as a result of going on this trip?

MISSION ACCOMPLISHED?

Aubrey sat in the back row of the fifteen-passenger van, awkwardly curled up with her legs on top of her backpack. The rest of the team was sleeping, heads leaning against windows and piles of pillows. Aubrey, though, was staring into the distance, exhausted but unable to sleep. She kept thinking of Michelle, a ten-year-old girl from Chicago she had befriended over the past six days. Images of her adorable grin played on repeat in her mind. Each morning, Aubrey and her fellow team members worked on houses in Michelle's neighborhood, and then ran VBS classes in the afternoon. Last night, Aubrey had to say goodbye. She tearfully gave Michelle a box of candy and school supplies. *It kills me to leave, but I know we both understand Jesus better because I was faithful to come here, sacrificing my time and resources to love her*, Aubrey thought as the van pulled into a filling station.

At first glance, it seems like Aubrey and her team successfully acted on their biblical command to love and serve people who are poor. After all, houses were freshly painted, and the neighborhood children had bracelets representing the gospel story the team had shared. But if Aubrey could spend months, or years, in that neighborhood, she would realize that alleviating poverty isn't that straightforward—her team may have recognized the symptoms of poverty, but there was actually something more happening beneath the surface.

WATCH

Close your books and watch this week's video via the QR code or link below.

www.helpingwithouthurting.org/stm-videos

Follow the prompts to set up an account or sign back in, utilizing the access code below to view the videos:

Code: COL120

DISCUSS

Initial Reflections

1. What are two or three ideas that struck you in the video? What questions do you have after seeing the video?

MAKING IT COUNT

Consider the following numbers and statistics:

- **2–3 million people:** 2010 estimate of how many people from the United States go on short-term mission trips (STMs) internationally each year[1]

- **20–25 percent:** The likelihood of any given church member going on an international STM sometime in their lifetime as of 2009[2]

- **$1,370–$1,450 per person:** Range of average cost for an international STM[3]

- **$1.6 *billion*:** A conservative estimate of international STM spending per year—that's $1,600,000,000[4]

- **4 million people:** number of the world's extreme poor whose *yearly* income would equal the $1.6 billion spent on international STMs in one year[5]

- **$3,000–$6,000 per year:** the range of *yearly* salary for a community-level relief and development worker in the Majority World—an STM of fifteen people at $1,400 per person would spend $21,000, an amount that could support three to seven staff members for a year

1. Out of the above numbers, what statistics surprise you the most? Why?

These numbers paint a sobering picture. Simply put, we spend a massive amount of money on short-term trips—money that could be used to support people working and ministering in their own communities, people who are already familiar with the context and culture of the community. These people could be used by God to evangelize, disciple, and combat poverty over the long haul.

2. Given this reality, how do you justify using God's money to go on this trip?

So why go? As we will see throughout these lessons, the purpose of a trip isn't primarily about what you will do or what impact you will have in two weeks. It's about what you can learn, in deep and meaningful ways, and how that learning can translate into long-term engagement in the world of missions and poverty alleviation.

REDEFINING POVERTY

How we define poverty will heavily influence how we respond to and attempt to alleviate that poverty. Take a moment to review the table below of commonly cited causes and responses to poverty:

If We Believe the Primary Cause of Poverty Is . . .	Then We Will Primarily Try to . . .
A Lack of Knowledge	Educate the Poor
Oppression by Powerful People	Work for Social Justice
The Personal Sins of the Poor	Evangelize and Disciple the Poor
A Lack of Material Resources	Give Material Resources to the Poor

1. Look back at your answers to the preliminary questions. Do your answers about poverty tend to emphasize one particular category above?

2. Which line(s) of the table above do you think short-term trips most frequently try to address, and how do they typically do it? Why do you think this is the case?

COMPLEXITY COUNTS

Because God is inherently relational and made humans in His image, humans are wired for relationship, too. When the four relationships are functioning properly, humans experience the fullness of life that God intended—we are being what God created us to be.

THE FOUR FOUNDATIONAL RELATIONSHIPS

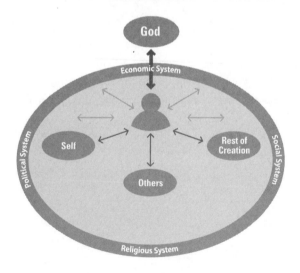

Adapted from Bryant L. Myers, *Walking with the Poor: Principles and Practices of Transformational Development* (Maryknoll, NY: Orbis Books, 1999), 27.

But as we discussed in the video, the fall broke these relationships.

THE FOUR BROKEN RELATIONSHIPS

Adapted from Bryant L. Myers, *Walking with the Poor: Principles and Practices of Transformational Development* (Maryknoll, NY: Orbis Books, 1999), 27.

From this framework, poverty isn't only about a lack of material things. While that is an important element of poverty, there are many other crucial factors at work. As a result, poverty—and poverty alleviation—is complex.

POVERTY

"Poverty is the result of relationships that do not work, that are not just, that are not for life, that are not harmonious or enjoyable. Poverty is the absence of shalom in all its meanings."

—Bryant Myers, *Walking with the Poor*[6]

Remember: because the fall impacted *everything*, both individual people and systems are broken. The brokenness in the four relationships means social, political, economic, and religious systems are marred by sin. Thus, poverty alleviation also involves transforming those systems. Sometimes people blame choices made by the materially poor for their poverty, arguing that anyone could escape poverty if they wanted to do so. While sinful individual choices can contribute to poverty, poverty is also the result of circumstances outside the control of the materially poor. For example, consider the prevalence of poverty in many US cities. Many neighborhoods bear the marks of centuries of racial discrimination and damaging economic, social, and political policies. What happens when society crams historically oppressed, undereducated, unemployed, and relatively young human beings into high-rise buildings, provides them with inferior education, healthcare, and employment systems, and then establishes financial disincentives for work? Is it really that surprising that we see out-of-wedlock pregnancies, broken families, violent crimes, and drug trafficking? Yes, those choices are still wrong. But they have a context. Both broken systems and broken individual choices contribute to poverty.

Part of the learning process of a short-term trip entails recalibrating our hearts and minds, moving away from easy—but incomplete and unbiblical—assumptions about the materially poor. Learning about and acknowledging the complexity of poverty, particularly in the community you will be visiting, is an essential part of long-term engagement in missions and poverty alleviation.

1. When you interact with the materially poor, do you tend to see their poverty more as a result of their personal actions or circumstances beyond their control?

- Would your answer to this question be different for the materially poor in your own community versus a community abroad? Why or why not?

2. Look back at how you described the purpose of your trip in the preliminary questions. Did part of your stated purpose involve poverty alleviation?

- If so, given the ideas on poverty and poverty alleviation in this unit, how might you need to adjust your expectations?

3. Given the complexity of poverty and poverty alleviation, how can you specifically commit to make this trip one part of a long-term process of learning and engagement in God's work, rather than a one-

time spiritual or emotional experience? Take a moment to discuss what these commitments and goals might look like for your group.

TAKEAWAYS

- Keep your eyes open for the ways poverty is influenced by broken relationships with God, self, others, and the rest of creation.

- Remember that poverty alleviation is not just a matter of providing people with material things. It is a process of reconciling the four foundational relationships. You are not participating in a short-term trip in order to directly alleviate poverty.

- View your trip as one piece of a long-term process of learning about, engaging with, and supporting God's work of missions and poverty alleviation.

CLOSE

Poverty is the result of broken relationships, and broken relationships can be restored by the work of Christ. He came to make all things new, breaking the hold of sin and death "far as the curse is found." He came to show us that we can have a relationship with our Father, that we have dignity as creatures made in God's image, that we are to love one another in nourishing community, and that we have the privilege of stewarding the rest of creation. The fall has marred what God intended for us at creation, but the work of Christ offers hope that what is broken, both inside of us and around us, will be repaired.

But that process doesn't happen in the space of a few days or weeks. If we are spending hundreds or thousands of dollars on a trip, we need a different set of goals, namely entering into a long-term, intentional process of learning about and engaging with what God is doing in our own country and around the globe—and supporting the people who *can* alleviate poverty in their own communities. It doesn't seem as tidy as digging wells, repairing houses, or running sports camps, but as we will see in the next few units, it can foster deeper change in both the receiving community and our own lives.

PRAY

"Every human being, regardless of income level, is made in the image of God, meaning that we are wired for relationship: with God, with ourselves, with others, and with the rest of creation. When we experience these four relationships in the way that God designed them, we experience humanness the way that He intended. This is the 'good life' that we are all seeking. Unfortunately, the fall has broken these four relationships for all people. For some, this brokenness manifests itself in material poverty."

Spend time this week praying that God would open your eyes to the complexity of poverty—and the magnitude of His reconciling power as He is making all things new. Pray that He would prepare your heart to see and support the work of your brothers and sisters who are already serving as ambassadors of reconciliation in their communities. And pray for humility as you consider what engaging with that work around the world and in your own community would look like.

NOTES

UNIT 2

WHO ARE THE **POOR?**

Discuss this question before beginning this week's unit.

• Take a moment to reflect on a time when you helped a materially poor person. What was going through your mind during and after you helped this person? What do you imagine was going through their mind?

WHAT'S THE GOAL?

"We've been sent to the least of these." "Taking back Africa for Jesus." "Hope for New Orleans." The taglines appear on brochures, T-shirts, and fundraising letters. Images of malnourished children or homeless people sleeping under overpasses star in short-term trip promotional videos. The appeals are emotionally compelling, and appear to be built around the biblical mandate to care for the materially poor. But on a deeper level, they say an enormous amount about how we view ourselves and how we view low-income people. As we saw in unit 1, poverty is rooted in the complexity of broken relationships. Then who are the poor? And what does poverty alleviation look like?

WATCH

Close your books and watch this week's video via the QR code or link below.

www.helpingwithouthurting.org/stm-videos

Follow the prompts to set up an account or sign back in, utilizing the access code below to view the videos:

Code: COL120

DISCUSS

Initial Reflections

1. What are two or three ideas that struck you in the video? What questions do you have after seeing the video?

OUR POVERTY

As discussed in the video, brokenness in the four relationships shapes all of us, not just the materially poor.

1. You may not be materially poor, but what evidence do you see in your life of brokenness in the four foundational relationships?

   • Relationship with God:

   • Relationship with Self:

   • Relationship with Others:

   • Relationship with the Rest of Creation:

Being aware of the way our own foundational relationships are marred by sin is crucial in fostering an attitude of humility. We are all dependent on the work of Christ in our lives, and we all share equal worth and value as His image-bearers. But as discussed in the video, the ways we experience poverty are fundamentally different. There is something uniquely devastating and painful about material poverty. The ways the materially rich experience poverty don't typically involve hunger pangs, watching family members die of malnutrition, or living in fear of violence outside our front doors. As we enter low-income communities, we must be very aware not to cheapen or delegitimize the pain that the materially poor endure by claiming to understand it, or that our experiences of brokenness are fully the same.

HELPING OR HURTING?

One of the biggest problems with short-term trips focused on poverty alleviation is that they can exacerbate the poverty of being of the economically rich—their god-complexes—and the poverty of being of the economically poor—their feelings of inferiority and shame.

Yes, we may help temporarily improve people's physical conditions. They may have clean water, repaired houses, or new classrooms. But other, powerful aspects of their poverty can be deepened. The equation below summarizes this dynamic:

Material Definition of Poverty		God-complexes of Materially Non-Poor		Feelings of Inferiority of Materially Poor		Harm to Both Materially Poor and Non-Poor
	+		+		=	

David Livermore, who has spent years studying cross-cultural engagement and short-term missions, shares a story that illustrates this dynamic. He and his wife, Linda, and their daughters were visiting Malaysia. After seeing a materially poor Malay father and daughter on the street, Livermore encouraged his own daughter to give the little girl a frog stuffed animal.

> As we started to leave, the Malay father ordered his daughter to return the frog. We motioned that we didn't want it back, but he insisted. He began to raise his voice and grabbed the frog and handed it to me. As I began to talk with Linda about it, we thought back to our home in the Chicago area. Though a beautiful house, our home was one of the more modest homes in our town. Linda asked, "So how would you feel if one of the parents in the million-dollar homes near us suddenly walked up to our girls and started handing them gifts?" All of a sudden I began to see this in a new light. I thought about how I would feel if some rich person started giving my girls unsolicited gifts in my presence. I'm quite capable of caring for them, thank you![1]

Livermore didn't anticipate that giving a simple stuffed animal—something he intended as an act of generosity—would provoke a negative response. Livermore's intentions were good, but he inadvertently angered and shamed the Malay father by implying that he could not adequately provide for his own child.

1. Have you ever seen this type of dynamic at work, whether in your own community or during a short-term trip? If so, how?

2. Look back at your answer to the preliminary question. In the situation you described, do you have any evidence to support what you think was going through the materially poor person's mind? How else might the materially poor recipient have perceived your help?

3. How might going on this trip help challenge you and heal you in areas of your brokenness?

4. How might going on this trip tempt you to further entrench areas of your brokenness?

TAKEAWAYS

• Remember that both the materially poor and materially rich experience brokenness in their four foundational relationships. You need Christ's reconciling work in your life, just as the materially poor do.

• Thus, remember that you are not going to "save" people who are poor. In fact, acting from a god-complex or arrogance-tainted heart is one of the fastest ways to harm the materially poor in our attempts to help them.

• Use Psalm 139:23–24 as an outline and central theme in prayer for this trip and learning process.

CLOSE

When we recognize that poverty is relational, *and that we are all poor*, we can enter a community with humility. We can guard against harming the materially poor with our god-complexes and arrogance, instead focusing our thoughts, actions, words, and attitudes on affirming the greatness of God, the dignity of the materially poor, and our mutual need for Christ. Rather than seeing ourselves as bringing hope to New Orleans or taking back Africa for Jesus, we can rejoice that Christ is already at work in these areas. Rather than seeing ourselves as saving "the least of these," we can celebrate together the ways the reconciling work of Christ is bringing healing to the poverty in *all of us.*

PRAY

"Who are the poor? We are the poor. When we truly believe this, when it shapes everything we say, think, and do, we can enter a materially poor community in humility. We can lay aside our drive to 'fix' the poor, we can put away our need to 'do' something, and instead we can open our hearts to learn from people who are poor, letting Christ restore both of us in our areas of brokenness."

Spend time praying together, reflecting on Psalm 139:23–24. Ask God to reveal the depths of your own sin and brokenness as you prepare for your trip. Pray that He would guard you against arrogance, using this process of learning and engagement to restore you to more of what He intended you to be.

NOTES

UNIT 3

THEY ARE NOT
HELPLESS

Discuss these questions before beginning this week's unit.

• In what contexts might you be willing to give low-income people things or money?

• In what contexts might you be uncomfortable giving low-income people things or money?

NOT ALL POVERTY IS CREATED EQUAL

After Hurricane Katrina wreaked havoc along parts of the Gulf Coast, tens of thousands of Christians rushed to assist, testifying to the beauty of the body of Christ. One particular youth short-term team arrived a few weeks after Katrina hit and cleared roads and homes of debris. The same group returned about a year later to help rehabilitate some of the damaged homes. The team spent days restoring a house owned by a family that included several young adult males. While the team worked hard every day tearing out Sheetrock, carpeting, and more, the young men living in the house sat back and watched the STM team. After the second trip, a few of the team members left unsettled—something didn't feel right. But why? Isn't all poverty created equal? After all, both trips were focused on serving the materially poor whom Hurricane Katrina had affected, and tasks and projects were successfully completed on both.

WATCH

Close your books and watch this week's video via the QR code or link below.

 www.helpingwithouthurting.org/stm-videos

Follow the prompts to set up an account or sign back in, utilizing the access code below to view the videos:

Code: COL120

DISCUSS

Initial Reflections

1. What are two or three ideas that struck you in the video? What questions do you have after seeing the video?

ONE OF THESE IS NOT LIKE THE OTHER

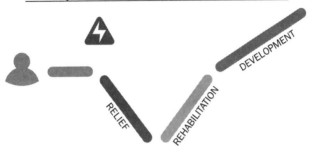

RELIEF, REHABILITATION, AND DEVELOPMENT

- **Relief**: An effort to "stop the bleeding." It is the urgent and temporary provision of emergency aid to reduce immediate suffering from a natural or man-made crisis, and it primarily utilizes a provider-receiver dynamic.

- **Rehabilitation**: An effort to restore people back to their pre-crisis state after the initial bleeding has stopped, while also laying the basis for future development. In rehabilitation, people begin to contribute to improving their situation.

- **Development**: Walking with people across time in ways that move all the people involved—both the "helpers" and the "helped"—closer to being in right relationship with God, self, others, and the rest of creation than they were before. This involves people identifying their problems, creating solutions, and implementing those solutions. Development is often referred to as "empowerment." It avoids "doing for" and focuses on "doing with."

Remember: The vast majority of materially poor communities and individuals require development, not relief or rehabilitation; they are not coming out of a crisis and they are not helpless. Rather, they are in a chronic state of poverty and have some ability to participate in their own progress.

Thus, a visual for development, which is the majority of poverty alleviation, is:

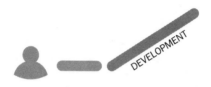

1. Look back at the preliminary questions to this unit. Would you retool your answers in light of the information about relief, rehabilitation, and development above? Why or why not?

IS THE GLASS HALF EMPTY OR HALF FULL?

1. Read the following verses. How might these verses inform the way we interact with the materially poor?

   • 1 Thessalonians 5:10–11:

• Philippians 4:8:

• 1 Corinthians 12:12–26:

• James 2:1–5:

Review the definitions of asset-based and needs-based development below.

NEEDS-BASED DEVELOPMENT
A development approach that focuses on the deficits and shortcomings in the life of a person or community; solutions to individual or community problems come from the outside

ASSET-BASED DEVELOPMENT
A development approach that focuses on identifying, mobilizing, and connecting the God-given capabilities, skills, and resources of a person or community to solve individual or community problems

Healthy, effective poverty alleviation approaches start by recognizing and celebrating the gifts and resources God has already placed in a community, whether natural resources, people, families, neighborhood associations, schools, businesses, governments, or individual skills. This isn't ignoring the problems that exist, but rather it is recognizing that there are assets available within a community and its people to attack the problems and create new opportunities. The exciting process of asset-based development is focused on identifying, mobilizing, and connecting these assets.

THE POISON OF PATERNALISM

Paternalism is habitually doing things for people that they can do for themselves.[1] Paternalism is slippery, though. It isn't just a matter of inappropriate handouts—it takes a number of subtle forms. Note the following variations of paternalism:

- **Resource Paternalism**: giving people resources they do not truly need and/or could acquire on their own

- **Spiritual Paternalism**: taking spiritual leadership away from the materially poor, assuming we have more to offer than they do

- **Knowledge Paternalism**: assuming we have all the best ideas about how to do things

- **Labor Paternalism**: doing work for the materially poor that they could do for themselves

- **Managerial Paternalism**: taking ownership of change away from the poor, insisting that they follow our "better, "more efficient" way of doing things

1. While you may have never experienced material poverty, consider experiences in your job, school, home, or church. Have you ever been on the receiving end of spiritual, managerial, or knowledge paternalism? How did those experiences make you feel?

2. Why do you think people are so quick to engage in paternalism, despite its negative effects?

3. Given the context of poverty that you will be experiencing on this visit, what type of asset-based interventions is the host ministry doing?

4. What actions by your group could support their success?

5. What actions by your group could hinder their success?

6. How might you specifically hold each other accountable to support, rather than hinder, successful ministry on this visit?

CLOSE

Not all poverty is created equal. Clearing debris after a hurricane and renovating houses for people a year later may seem like similarly valid responses to poverty. But context is everything. We have a responsibility to not harm a community when we enter it, and to not undermine the long-term poverty alleviation work already being done. We love *doing* things, and we forget that the materially poor are not helpless. There are times when more or less assistance is needed. But they are ultimately created in the image of God with unique gifts and capacities. We dare not rob them of that dignity through our efforts to do and accomplish particular tasks. Instead, as we will explore in the following units, we have an opportunity to learn from them and affirm their dignity through short-term trips.

TAKEAWAYS

- Do not give money or material things to the people you encounter. If you desire to help, then approach the host organization and allow them to determine how the resources can be best used.

- Avoid paternalism: do not do things for the materially poor that they are capable of doing for themselves. You may have opportunities to work *alongside* community members on a task that they have initiated and are executing, blessing them with your company and additional labor. But involvement should always be under their leadership and participation.

- Rather than fixating on the material needs you see, look for the gifts God has already placed in the community and in individuals.

PRAY

"If you go back to the definition of poverty, poverty alleviation isn't just about fixing the materially poor's circumstances. It is about helping them discover that they are an image-bearer and that they have tremendous value as a human being, that they are called to be a steward of their resources and opportunities. When we visit a community, we have to be incredibly careful that we respect that process, not undermine it."

Pray for the work that God is already doing in the community you will be visiting. Pray that God would give you open eyes and hearts to recognize that work and to see the gifts He has given the materially poor. Ask for wisdom as you enter the community, coming alongside your brothers and sisters as they engage in the long-term process of poverty alleviation.

NOTES

UNIT 4

THE KINGDOM IS
UPSIDE **DOWN**

Discuss these questions before beginning this week's unit.

• Has there ever been a time when someone sought out your wisdom or opinion, wanting to learn from your experiences? How did this make you feel?

• Has there ever been a time when someone was willing to enter into your life, listening to you share aspects of your heart and reality? How did this make you feel?

43

WHAT NOW?

If poverty alleviation is a long-term process and can't be achieved by simply providing material things to people who are poor, then what is the purpose of a short-term trip? If trips focused on "doing" or "fixing" things often cause harm, then on what are we called to focus? Consider the following story from David Livermore:

> A group from my church just returned from a couple weeks in Rwanda. Within their first hour in Rwanda, the local team said, "Ninety percent of your job is done. You're here, your presence speaks volumes." One of the team members told me she thought, "Well, I don't think so. That's gracious of you, but we're here to work hard." The longer she was there, however, the more she began to see that the tasks they came to do were not what was needed most. The presence and chance for relationship together seemed to be the most pressing need for the Rwandan church beyond any menial tasks that were planned.[1]

When done well, a short-term trip is just one step in the long-term process of Jesus Christ remaking both the materially poor and those of us who want to help. Within that framework, our presence can be a powerful blessing, and what we learn during our time can create opportunities for transformation down the road.

WATCH

Close your books and watch this week's video via the QR code or link below.

   www.helpingwithouthurting.org/stm-videos

Follow the prompts to set up an account or sign back in, utilizing the access code below to view the videos:

Code: COL120

DISCUSS

Initial Reflections

1. What are two or three ideas that struck you in the video? What questions do you have after seeing the video?

WHAT LEARNING, FELLOWSHIP, AND ENCOURAGEMENT CAN LOOK LIKE

1. Read 1 Corinthians 1:26–31 and Colossians 4:7–16. How might these passages provide a foundation for engaging in learning, fellowship, and encouragement as we enter a low-income community?

• Now think back to the ways the materially poor and non-poor are broken. How could entering a community with a 1 Corinthians 1 attitude begin to address the brokenness in both of our hearts?

The idea that learning, fellowship, and encouragement are legitimate purposes for a short-term trip within the context of long-term engagement can seem strange at first. Take a moment to read the accounts below:

Our groups would sit on an open-air porch around a single table for dinner, and various members of the community would join us four or five times throughout the week. The guests were very different— farmers, pastors, students, or housewives. One at a time, they would eat with us and we would all swap stories and small talk. After supper, they would share about their worlds. The teacher would talk about the educational challenges in the community. The pastor would talk about spiritual warfare. The student would explain his or her typical day, how he or she would walk three to four miles to school or do homework by candlelight. . . . Other times, we would arrange for team members to attend church services that just met in community members' front yards. We wanted participants to see and understand how the local church was already proclaiming God's excellencies and ministering to one another.

—Michael and Shelley, former full-time missionaries[2]

I was leading a team of youth on a short-term trip to a very secular part of Europe. We had anticipated the primary focus being projects on the church building, or outreach to the low-income community around the church. Instead, when we got there, the pastor greeted the team and said, "All I care about is that you have breakfast, lunch, and dinner with members of our church every day. This isn't the easiest place to be a Christian—there aren't tons of passionate believers around us. I want your presence and passion to be refreshing to our church." At first, I found the notion strange. Eating meals with church members? But then I realized, "What a beautiful example of what a short-term trip can be."

—Marco Perez, former team leader and team host[3]

The following story is from Jason, who has led trips as part of long-term engagement with orphans, many of whom are now young adults:

I never understood the place of lament in our faith [before]. One night during a praise service, several of the youth just broke down crying, and then doubled over screaming. They began sobbing, "Why, why, why," and "It hurts, it hurts, it hurts," and "Why did they leave me?" It was gut-wrenching. We didn't know how to process that. It sent us, as a team and congregation, on years of exploring what worship looks like out of a context of pain and distress. None of that was in the gospel that we consciously brought with us to that community. But it is a part of the gospel that the Spirit led us to through our relationships with them. We read our Bibles, especially the Psalms, in new ways. . . . Because of these types of encounters, some participants have even pursued formal training in trauma therapy and counseling. They are now using that training in our own community and as we continue to walk alongside our brothers and sisters overseas.[4]

1. What strikes you about the underlying values and attitudes expressed in these stories and quotes?

2. How do you feel now about having learning, fellowship, and encouragement as the core purposes of this visit?

TAKEAWAYS

• You must be committed to learning about the historical, social, political, and spiritual context of the community you will be visiting, and seek to better understand the complex causes and manifestations of poverty in the area.

• During this visit, be ready to look for specific ways that you can learn from the materially poor's experiences and wisdom. Be open to ways God may use them to confront or address areas of sin and brokenness in your own heart.

• Remember: as you learn from and fellowship with your brothers and sisters, constantly consider what your long-term role is in engaging with and supporting effective poverty alleviation and missions—both around the world and in your own community.

CLOSE

God does not call His children because they are exceptional. He does not choose the perfect, the wealthy, or the influential. No one has grounds to boast, and none of us are at the "top" in His kingdom. When we enter a low-income community and prioritize learning, fellowship, and encouragement, we are recognizing that God chooses the "foolish things of the world to shame the wise" and "the weak things of the world to shame the strong" (1 Corinthians 1:27). Instead of focusing on accomplishing projects and tasks, we enter into a refrain of humble praise: "Let us boast in the Lord together! Let us celebrate the things He has done in our lives through Christ!" In the process, we leave our hearts open to Christ as He remakes us, leading us toward long-term, deeply transformative ways of joining in His work.

PRAY

"When we pause, setting the shovels down and putting the puppets away, we realize that the materially poor have an incredible amount to teach us about God, the kingdom, and ourselves. In return, we have the privilege of humbly coming alongside the work God is doing through them, supporting them and engaging with them in work that we could never do as outsiders. And that's a beautiful thing."

Spend time in prayer, asking God to give you a heart of profound humility and openness to what He has for you to learn. And pray that He would give you sensitivity to how you can best bless and encourage His people working in the community, loving your brothers and sisters well.

NOTES

UNIT 5

BEING A **BLESSING**

Discuss these questions before beginning this week's unit.

• Describe a time when someone misunderstood your words or actions. What was at the root of the misunderstanding?

• Describe a time when you felt disrespected by someone. Why did you feel this way?

DANCING CAREFULLY

As we build trips around learning, fellowship, and encouragement, we still have to be very conscientious when interacting with our hosts. Missions expert Miriam Adeney relates a story told to her by an African Christian friend:

> Elephant and Mouse were best friends. One day Elephant said, "Mouse, let's have a party!" Animals gathered from far and near. They ate, and drank, and sang, and danced. And nobody celebrated more exuberantly than the Elephant. After it was over, Elephant exclaimed, "Mouse, did you ever go to a better party? What a celebration!" But Mouse did not answer. "Where are you?" Elephant called. Then he shrank back in horror. There at his feet lay the Mouse, his body ground into the dirt—smashed by the exuberance of his friend, the Elephant. "Sometimes that is what it is like to do mission with you Westerners," the African storyteller commented. "It is like dancing with an Elephant."[1]

Thankfully, there are ways we can prepare to dance well during our visits, seeking to support and bless our hosts more effectively.

WATCH

Close your books and watch this week's video via the QR code or link below.

 www.helpingwithouthurting.org/stm-videos

Follow the prompts to set up an account or sign back in, utilizing the access code below to view the videos:

Code: COL120

DISCUSS

Initial Reflections

1. What are two or three ideas that struck you in the video? What questions do you have after seeing the video?

NO SUCH THING AS "NORMAL"

1. Review the definition of "cultural norms" below.

CULTURAL NORMS

Subconscious assumptions, behaviors, and protocols that people naturally follow without even thinking about them

2. Have you ever personally encountered a different set of cultural norms, whether in another country, another church, or even another family setting? If so, how did you respond?

3. Referencing resource module B, your leader will now talk you through some of the basic differences in the cultural norms below. What three norms appear to pose the biggest difference between your culture and the receiving culture?

• Concept of Time:

• Concept of Self:

• Role of Face/Degree of Directness:

• Locus of Control:

• Power Distance:

4. Take a moment to imagine a situation in which a differing norm could cause problems or present challenges on your trip. How might you handle this situation wisely, respecting your hosts?

5. What might be the implications of the following passages on respecting our brothers and sisters and respecting cultural differences?

• Philippians 2:1–11:

• Ephesians 4:1–6:

LEAVING DONALD AT HOME

When we, as middle-to-upper-class people, walk into a low-income community—particularly in the Majority World—everything we say carries more weight than we intend. As a result, we can undermine local participation and initiative in development and ministry work. It also means that our displeasure or frustrations can be magnified, causing extra insult and damage.

1. Have you ever been on the receiving end of the Donald Trump Effect, whether in your church, office, or family?

2. Have you ever been pushed toward a particular action because of someone's resources, influence, or status? If so, how did it make you feel?

3. Are you mentally, emotionally, and spiritually prepared to take a backseat to local workers and believers, supporting their work at the expense of a feeling of contributing to helping people who are poor?

PICTURING DIGNITY

We live in a culture where every latte, sunset, or family gathering is fair game for a picture or social media post. For many of us, it is a way of sharing and documenting our day-to-day lives. But we need to be aware of how our love for photography and social media may play out on a short-term trip. Take a moment to discuss the following questions:

1. How would you feel if you were walking in your neighborhood and someone drove by taking pictures of you?

2. What if a stranger walked into your church and started taking pictures of your children, nieces or nephews, or younger siblings, posting these pictures on the Internet for the world to see? How would you feel?

When we enter a low-income community, we have to adjust our habits and ask ourselves whether we are "doing unto others" well. The stories we are hearing and the scenes we are seeing aren't ours to share with the rest of the world automatically. We have to respect the dignity and privacy of the people we encounter, including through our photography. A picture of a hurting, vacant-eyed mother may be emotionally compelling, but it doesn't prioritize her dignity. A picture of you with malnourished, needy-looking children may make for a great profile pic, but it can treat those children and families as a spectacle. Before you snap a picture, ask yourself the following questions:

• Does this picture communicate and emphasize the God-given gifts and dignity of the materially poor, or does it flatten them into a one-dimensional caricature of pain and desperation?

• Does this picture paint me as saving, rescuing, or fixing the materially poor or their community in any way?

- How would I feel if outsiders depicted me or my community in this way? Am I "doing unto others" well?

Further, your trip leader may prohibit social media use while you are on the field. Be fully present, setting aside the desire to document a moment in favor of creating a safe space for personal interaction. Live in the rhythm of the community, removing the mental and emotional distraction of keeping up with home. Your trip leader can and will keep your families updated. So unplug. You will learn more if you do.

Here are a few general guidelines to follow while you are on the field:

- Do not take pictures during conversations, worship gatherings, or visiting someone's home.

- Ask permission before taking pictures of or with people, and be extremely cautious of taking pictures of or with children.

- If you do use social media during the trip, limit it to evenings and run a draft post by a team member, discussing whether it is dignity-affirming or not.

TAKEAWAYS

- Assume things are more complex than meets the eye. Be very slow to make assumptions about people, situations, attitudes, or problems.

- Carefully listen to and obey instructions from your local hosts, respecting their procedures, behavioral guidelines, and cultural advice.

- Be flexible. Recognize that plans and logistics during your trip will most likely change or be upended at a moment's notice. Be prepared to go with the flow, rather than expecting things to go a certain way.

- Be extremely hesitant to make "suggestions" or share your opinions. Remember: your hosts know more about living in their communities than you ever could. You are not the experts.

- Be very cautious about photography and social media usage. "Do unto others" well.

CLOSE

Visiting a new context and culture can be disorienting and overwhelming, particularly if we feel the pressure to accomplish something or have a particular experience. As we have discussed, moving away from an emphasis on "doing" allows us to dance well on short-term trips, reframing the visit as an opportunity to learn from, fellowship with, and encourage our hosts. But more than anything, remember that your trip is one piece in a long-term process of learning and engagement. Don't feel pressure to have a profound experience each day. Don't force an incident or story to have immediate meaning. Yes, be thoughtful and observant. But remember: snap judgments and assumptions typically lead us to faulty conclusions.

You will record your experiences throughout your trip in unit 6. You will then reflect on and analyze those experiences when you return home, setting concrete goals about how you will steward your trip and engage as you move forward. So take the long view, and don't expect the trip itself to be a revolutionary experience. In fact, by itself, the trip probably will not create concrete, lasting change in your life. It's what you do when you return, and the ongoing work of the Holy Spirit, that fosters long-term growth and transformation.

PRAY

"Ultimately, we have a responsibility to 'do unto others' well. Yes, these kinds of contextual and cultural differences can complicate that process. But that's why we start with listening. We start with learning. We start with just being with our brothers and sisters. And we trust that God will work in and through that process, opening new, mutually edifying ways for us to serve and to support one another."

Pray that God would grant you and your team wisdom as you enter an unfamiliar community. Pray that He would give you sensitivity to opportunities to effectively bless the people you meet, and that He would prompt your heart at any moments where your own god-complexes might be tainting those interactions.

NOTES

UNIT 6

ON THE **GROUND**[1]

OBSERVATION CATEGORIES

Skim over the topics below each evening, jotting down any stories or observations that relate to these ideas. You will return to these observations after your trip to think about and discuss them further. Don't feel like you need to write an essay each night. Use brief bullet points or keywords. Think of the below categories as buckets to help gather and sort your experiences, ensuring that you don't forget the things you observed.

• Different aspects of broken relationships and material poverty

- Examples of effective and ineffective poverty alleviation (healthy development work vs. inappropriate relief efforts, the materially poor participating in their own improvement vs. the temptations and dangers of paternalism, etc.)

- Seeing the materially poor through the lens of their God-given gifts and assets, not their needs or deficits

- The beauty of learning from, fellowshiping with, and encouraging our brothers and sisters, even those the world would call "weak"

• Respecting the culture and leaders of the receiving community

• Learning about and recognizing the systemic causes of ¨poverty, such as economic, social, or political factors, in a particular area.

TRACKING QUESTIONS

Each evening, take a moment to look at the questions below. Using bullet points, jot down answers under the questions. Expand on your thoughts and stories as much as you would like, but don't feel pressure to write long paragraphs. You will return to these observations later.

Date:

1. Briefly recap your day. How did you spend your time, and with whom did you interact?

2. What was the highlight of your day—what was the most exciting, interesting, or energizing moment?

3. What was the hardest part of your day—what was the most saddening, confusing, or frustrating moment?

4. Did today's experiences leave you with any: A) Questions or areas you would like to understand more deeply? or B) Ideas about how you can engage with and support poverty alleviation as you return home?

Date:

1. Briefly recap your day. How did you spend your time, and with whom did you interact?

2. What was the highlight of your day—what was the most exciting, interesting, or energizing moment?

3. What was the hardest part of your day—what was the most saddening, confusing, or frustrating moment?

4. Did today's experiences leave you with any: A) Questions or areas you would like to understand more deeply? or B) Ideas about how you can engage with and support poverty alleviation as you return home?

Date:

1. Briefly recap your day. How did you spend your time, and with whom did you interact?

2. What was the highlight of your day—what was the most exciting, interesting, or energizing moment?

3. What was the hardest part of your day—what was the most saddening, confusing, or frustrating moment?

4. Did today's experiences leave you with any: A) Questions or areas you would like to understand more deeply? or B) Ideas about how you can engage with and support poverty alleviation as you return home?

Date:

1. Briefly recap your day. How did you spend your time, and with whom did you interact?

2. What was the highlight of your day—what was the most exciting, interesting, or energizing moment?

3. What was the hardest part of your day—what was the most saddening, confusing, or frustrating moment?

4. Did today's experiences leave you with any: A) Questions or areas you would like to understand more deeply? or B) Ideas about how you can engage with and support poverty alleviation as you return home?

Date:

1. Briefly recap your day. How did you spend your time, and with whom did you interact?

2. What was the highlight of your day—what was the most exciting, interesting, or energizing moment?

3. What was the hardest part of your day—what was the most saddening, confusing, or frustrating moment?

4. Did today's experiences leave you with any: A) Questions or areas you would like to understand more deeply? or B) Ideas about how you can engage with and support poverty alleviation as you return home?

Date:

1. Briefly recap your day. How did you spend your time, and with whom did you interact?

2. What was the highlight of your day—what was the most exciting, interesting, or energizing moment?

3. What was the hardest part of your day—what was the most saddening, confusing, or frustrating moment?

4. Did today's experiences leave you with any: A) Questions or areas you would like to understand more deeply? or B) Ideas about how you can engage with and support poverty alleviation as you return home?

Date:

1. Briefly recap your day. How did you spend your time, and with whom did you interact?

2. What was the highlight of your day—what was the most exciting, interesting, or energizing moment?

3. What was the hardest part of your day—what was the most saddening, confusing, or frustrating moment?

4. Did today's experiences leave you with any: A) Questions or areas you would like to understand more deeply? or B) Ideas about how you can engage with and support poverty alleviation as you return home?

FINAL EVENING REFLECTIONS[2]

During your final group meeting on the field, spend time discussing the below questions.

1. Jot down what you would consider the top two highlights of this trip. What made these highlights?

2. Reflect on what the most difficult part of this trip was for you. Why do you think it was so hard?

3. What are some ways you can continue the process of learning and engagement when you return home, supporting the work you visited and effective poverty alleviation in your own community? Jot down some initial goals for how you will steward this experience, making it one piece of a long-term process. You will revisit these goals when you return home, but for now, share the first few things that come to mind.

4. When people ask you about your trip when you return home, what will you tell them? Take several minutes to write a couple of sentences describing the purpose of the trip, what you learned, and how you will now be exploring what deeper engagement in effective poverty alleviation might look like.

5. What are specific ways your team can pray for you as you return home? Take time to pray for each other, the community you have visited, the brothers and sisters you have met, and the work that God is doing.

6. Look over unit 7, and begin thinking about how you would respond to those questions. Before your first post-trip meeting, jot down your thoughts in unit 7, preparing to share your ideas with your team.

NOTES

UNIT 7

UNPACKING

- Take a moment and share what you have felt and experienced as you have returned home. Are there moments that you have found awkward or difficult? If so, how and why?

- Is there a particular moment or person on your trip that you have found yourself thinking of more than any other? If so, share it.

REFLECT

Jot down basic thoughts to the following questions before coming to your first post-trip meeting. At the meeting, share your ideas, referencing your on-field journaling to inform your discussion.

UNDERSTANDING POVERTY ALLEVIATION

1. What struck you or surprised you about what effective poverty alleviation looks like on a practical level? Were there elements of poverty alleviation that were more complex than you realized before your trip?

2. Reflect on the work of the organization or ministry that hosted your team. In what ways did you see the principles of asset-based, participatory development at work?

3. Did you see any paternalism evident in your own heart and actions? If so, how did you go about addressing it during the course of the trip?

• Did you see any paternalism at work in the broader community you visited? If so, what forms (labor, resource, knowledge, spiritual, and/or managerial) did you observe?

LEARNING FROM THE MATERIALLY POOR

1. What personal, spiritual, physical, and social assets or strengths did you see in the local community?

• In what ways did your presence support and celebrate the God-given gifts in the community?

2. How did you specifically and deliberately submit to the leadership of the local leaders?

• Were there any moments when you struggled to respect and follow the direction of your hosts? If so, when and why? How did you navigate those moments?

3. Reflect on your interactions with local people. What did you learn from their experiences and stories? What challenged you? What encouraged you?

4. Think back to your times of fellowship with local believers. Did spending time with your brothers and sisters impact the way you view your faith, the church, and/or the kingdom of God? If so, how?

UNDERSTANDING THEIR WORLD

1. What cultural differences did you encounter during your visit? Were there any tense moments because of cultural differences, particularly regarding the cultural norms you studied before your trip?

• If so, how did you navigate these moments?

• What strengths did you see in the receiving community's culture?

2. In what ways did you see individual choices contributing to poverty in the receiving community? In what ways did you see systemic factors—circumstances outside of the control of a materially poor person—contribute to poverty?

3. Reflect on poverty in your own community. Are there any ways in which your experience on your trip might inform the way you view the materially poor in your own context?

PROCESSING MUTUAL POVERTY

1. In what ways did the trip reveal areas of brokenness in your own four relationships?

2. What might it look like for you to more fully rely on Christ's reconciling work in your life in these areas?

CLOSE

The visit you just experienced was a gift. The world has shrunk remarkably in the space of a few decades, creating new opportunities to engage with the body of Christ and see the work God is doing through His people. The apostle Paul spent his life sailing around the Mediterranean world visiting churches, often arriving shipwrecked, waterlogged, or snakebitten. Early believers, or even the missionaries of 150 years ago, could never have dreamed of boarding an airplane or bus and traveling as freely and easily as you just did. *But more than a gift, this trip was an investment.* God has entrusted you with this opportunity. So embrace your responsibility to continue the process of learning and engagement. Move forward with a humble heart, seeking how and where God would have you apply this experience to your heart and in your own community.

PRAY

"Search me, God, and know my heart;
    test me and know my anxious thoughts.
See if there is any offensive way in me,
    and lead me in the way everlasting."

—Psalm 139:23-24

Spend time in prayer, asking God to continually reveal areas of your heart in need of His healing work. And pray for humility and perseverance, asking God to give you a teachable heart as you consider what applying and stewarding this experience looks like.

NOTES

UNIT 8

MAKING IT **COUNT**

Discuss the following questions before beginning this week's unit.

• Take a moment to reflect once more on all that your trip cost. What was the monetary cost? How much time did members of the receiving community dedicate to hosting you?

• Two years from now, how would you like to answer the following question: "How did your visit lead to positive change in materially poor communities?"

IT ISN'T OVER

You prepared for your trip well. You did your best to learn from, respect, and encourage your hosts. But a few simple facts remain: An international short-term trip costs an average of $1,370–$1,450 per person.[1] The range of *yearly* salary for a community-level relief and development worker in the Majority World is $3,000–6,000. That means the money spent on a team of fifteen people could support three to seven local staff members for a year. One missionary, when asked about the amount of time it takes to prepare, host, and recover from hosting a team, estimated that it took four weeks of work time.[2]

Your job isn't done yet. How will you steward and build upon the dollars, hours, and effort *invested in you*? How will you allow your experience to shape the way you engage with God's work in the world and with your materially poor brothers and sisters? While the Holy Spirit is the ultimate author of change in our hearts, we have a responsibility to be active participants in that process. So how will you make this experience count?

WATCH

Close your books and watch this week's video via the QR code or link below.

 www.helpingwithouthurting.org/stm-videos

Follow the prompts to set up an account or sign back in, utilizing the access code below to view the videos:

Code: COL120

DISCUSS

Initial Reflections

1. What are two or three ideas that struck you in the video? What questions do you have after seeing the video?

MAKING A CHANGE

1. Take a moment to read Philippians 2:4–13. What might this passage say about how we should view obedience and the process of change in our lives?

In light of these truths, take a moment to review the list of possible avenues for long-term engagement below:

• **Pray** faithfully for the community and people you visited, for your own community, and for wisdom as you continue to learn about and engage in God's work in the world.

• **Advocate** for the specific ministry or organization you visited, telling others the story of what God is doing. As part of this process, stay connected with the region and community you visited via newsletters from the host organization and broader current events that impact the community.

• **Financially support** the specific ministry or organization you visited, enabling them to continue ministering in their own community.

- **Support effective ministry** in your own community through your prayers, finances, time, and encouragement.

- **Support the leadership** of your church as they develop healthy partnerships and engage in effective poverty alleviation both in your own community and around the world.

- **Be a loving voice** in your congregation for effective poverty alleviation approaches.

2. Can you think of any other things you would add to the list above? If so, what?

3. Look back at the initial goals you described on your last day on the field (end of unit 6.) In light of those goals, your answer to the second preliminary question, and the list above, discuss three ways you might more deeply engage with and support what God is doing.

4. One of the most important factors in implementing change is setting effective goals. A common acronym for goal-setting is SMART. This means goals should be Specific, Measurable, Area-specific, Realistic, and Time-bound. Building on your answers above, write out two SMART goals for further engagement. For each goal, commit to steps and time frames below.

• In the next two months, I will:

• In the next six months, I will:

• In the next year, I will:

5. You will be meeting monthly or bimonthly to check in with your group. But take a moment to discuss how you might specifically hold each other accountable to these goals between meetings.

POTENTIAL HANG-UPS

Take a moment to review the list of obstacles short-term trip participants often face following their experience:

• Putting their experience on the shelf, leaving it to be a one-time emotional or spiritual high

• Becoming an STM consumer, taking repeated trips to enjoy the spiritual high without implementing change in their daily lives

• Becoming arrogant, thinking that they are superior to others because of what they have seen, learned, or experienced

1. Are there any other obstacles that you can imagine encountering? If so, what?

2. Of the obstacles above, which do you think will be particularly tempting or problematic for you?

• What steps could you take to guard yourself from experiencing this obstacle, and how can your team pray for you in that process?

REPORTING BACK

You have a responsibility to communicate to your prayer and financial supporters how you are stewarding their investment. Create a follow-up letter to send to these supporters that answers the following questions:

• What are the things you are learning as a result of this long-term process?

• What were some of the ways that you supported and encouraged your hosts while you were there?

• What was the highlight of the visit, and what was the most stretching part of the visit?

• What are the specific steps you are taking and seeking to take in order to convert this experience into lasting change in your life and ongoing engagement with God's work?

• What ways can your supporters continue to pray for you and the community you visited?

1. Discuss as a team the date by which you will send this letter to your supporters.

At your next team meeting, you will hold each other accountable for writing and sending this letter. Further, if you are presenting anything to your church about this journey, use the above questions as an outline for your presentation.

NEXT STEPS SUMMARY

Compile your reflections above into a concrete plan.

1. I am committing to stay engaged in the work I saw and what God is doing in my own community by:

2. The top obstacle I need to be aware of as I pursue these goals is:

3. I will send my follow-up letter to supporters by:

4. Our next check-in meeting as a team is on:

TAKEAWAYS

- Return to your "Next Steps Summary" on a weekly or biweekly basis, reminding yourself of the goals you created for ongoing engagement.

- Keep in touch with your team members, encouraging and holding each other accountable for stewarding your experiences and following through on your goals.

- Pray that God would grant you perseverance, focus, and diligence in the process of stewarding your trip, remembering that God is the one who is ultimately at work in your heart.

CLOSE

Over the past several months, you have learned about the principles of poverty alleviation, the beauty of culture, and what God is doing in another community. You have traveled to see that work, to meet with your brothers and sisters, and explore how you can best love and support them. And hopefully God has opened your eyes to your own need of Him, leaving you with an incredible longing for His reconciling power to heal the brokenness in and around you.

Foster that longing and join that work. Jesus Christ is indeed making all things new, and it is our great privilege to be part of that process. Remember that you aren't alone in longing for glimpses of Christ's ultimate restoration to invade the brokenness of this world, for the good news of the gospel to be proclaimed and demonstrated among people who are poor. The brothers and sisters you visited, and the very people sitting next to you, stand with you in that longing. And most importantly, that longing itself is the Spirit working in and through you.

Day by day and year by year, dig deeper in to the depth and breadth of God's work in the world. Build on what you have experienced, using it as a catalyst for your own transformation and the transformation of others. Steward the opportunity well, and rejoice that God is faithful to complete what He has begun.

PRAY

"What happens as you move forward is the single biggest factor in whether your trip was worth it. You just encountered both the pain of material poverty and hopefully the beauty of Christ's reconciling work in a new way. But you know that this excitement of the experience of the trip itself will be short-lived. Change happens when we prayerfully and purposefully convert your trip experience into a deep joy about the kingdom of God and the privilege it is to be a part of His work in the world."

Spend time in prayer for the community you visited and for the brothers and sisters you encountered. Pray that God would give you the endurance to pursue lasting engagement with His work, resting in the power of the Holy Spirit bring forth fruit in your life.

Use these questions during your monthly or bimonthly accountability and encouragement meetings.

1. Have you had any new reflections, insights, or questions about your trip since the group last met?

   • Have you found yourself thinking about or seeing particular experiences in your daily life differently as a result of your trip? If so, share examples.

2. Reflect back on your goals and obstacles from unit 8:

   • What has been going well?

   • What has been difficult?

3. In what areas would you like to grow, whether by incorporating a new goal or improving on a current goal?

4. How can your team pray for you as the Holy Spirit continues to work in your heart and as you seek to engage more deeply with God's work in the world?

RESOURCE MODULE A: FUNDRAISING

Pursuing a trip focused on long-term engagement, learning, fellowship, and encouragement should also impact how we fund our trips. Given the incredible amount of financial resources invested in a trip, we have a responsibility to communicate to donors what the trip will be and how we are committed to making the trip worth the financial investment. To that end, here are some general principles for raising support:

- You need to personally contribute to the cost of your trip. In the same way that the materially poor are more likely to "own" their own poverty alleviation and improvement if they have a personal and financial stake in the activities, you are more likely to steward this opportunity well if you have invested your own hard-earned cash in the trip. Your leader will work with you to determine what level of personal investment will be appropriate.

- You need to be realistic with your supporters about what you will be doing on this trip and what you won't be doing. Recognize that the trip costs significant financial resources, and make it clear how you plan to make their investment count over the long-term.

- Use this as an opportunity to advocate for the ministry you are visiting. Highlight the long-term work they are doing and how God is already at work through them. Make it clear that the purpose of this trip is to come alongside them.

Consider the following sample fundraising letter:

Dear _____,

I hope you are well, and that you are enjoying the onset of spring. As someone who has invested so much in me over the years, I wanted to let you know about an opportunity I have this summer.

A small group of people from my church, Deer Creek Church, has committed to an eight- to ten-month process of learning about poverty and appropriate poverty alleviation strategies. This involves fully participating in two months of preparatory meetings, a one-week trip, and multiple meetings over six to eight months after the trip. We will be traveling to Philadelphia, PA from July 10–July 17 to be with our brothers and sisters at Peace Fellowship Church. For the past fifteen years, PFC has been actively involved in ministry and poverty alleviation in its community. They started by working with local schools to support and staff after-school tutoring programs, developing relationships with low-income students and their families. PFC's community was heavily impacted by the 2008 recession, which led to even higher unemployment rates. Thus, PFC has developed financial education and jobs preparedness ministries in its community, helping individuals and families support themselves and find dignity through work.

PFC recognizes that poverty is about more than just a lack of material things. They are digging deep into the community, developing relationships with neighborhood leaders and members and walking with them over time as they move out of poverty. I realize that I can't do in seven days what has taken them years to do. As a result, instead of focusing on completing particular projects, here are my goals for my time in Philadelphia:

- Exploring how God is calling me to engage with missions and poverty alleviation as I continue to grow.

- Assisting and supporting PFC in whatever way they desire while we are there.

- Spending time with PFC staff and the residents of their neighborhood, observing the work God is already doing in their community and learning from their experiences.

- Encouraging and fellowshiping with my brothers and sisters in Christ, learning how I can best pray for and support their work over time.

Would you please join me in praying for PFC, the community members, and the team of people from my church? Pray that God will continue to open up new avenues and opportunities for PFC to demonstrate the hope of the gospel, and that our team would be humble encouragers and supporters as we enter their community.

Further, would you pray about contributing to the financial requirements of this trip? I realize that asking you to invest your God-given resources in a trip focused on learning from and fellowshiping with community members may seem strange. However, I take your investment seriously. In fact, I am dedicating some of my own money to the cost of the trip. You see, I am committed to making this trip one piece of a process of learning and action. Along with my teammates, I will be exploring how to support, engage with, and foster effective ministry and poverty alleviation efforts like PFC's—whether in my own community or across the globe.

Please return the enclosed card if you would like to receive prayer updates before and after the trip. Further, if you would like to invest in this trip financially, please enclose a check to Deer Creek Church with my name and "PFC Trip" in the memo line. The total cost of the trip will be $600, which will include bus transportation, lodging, and most of my meals. If you choose to give financially, it would be helpful for planning purposes to have any contributions by May 15.

Thank you so much for your time and the many ways you have been a part of my life. I look forward to seeing what God has in store for this summer and beyond, and it is a privilege to have people like you come alongside me in that process.

In Christ,

Maria

RESOURCE MODULE B: CULTURAL NORMS

CULTURAL NORMS

Subconscious assumptions, behaviors, and protocols that people naturally follow without even thinking about them

Concept of Time: *What is time, and how is it to be used?*

• Monochronic Cultures: Time is a limited resource that must be used carefully, so you need to save time and not waste time. Punctuality and efficiency reign supreme.

• Polychronic Cultures: Time is nebulous and almost limitless. There is always more time, so relationships trump efficiency.

Concept of Time

Adapted from Craig Storti, *Figuring Foreigners Out: A Practical Guide* (Yarmouth, ME: Intercultural Press, 1999), 82.

Concept of Self: *What is "self," and where does it find importance?*

• Individualistic Cultures: Identity is found in being unique, and success is "being all you can be" by exercising freedom of choice. Independence is a core value.

• Collectivist Cultures: Identity is found in being a part of a broader group and success is knowing and fulfilling your role in the group. Interdependence is a core value.

Concept of Self

Adapted from Craig Storti, *Figuring Foreigners Out: A Practical Guide* (Yarmouth, ME: Intercultural Press, 1999), 52.

Face and Directness: *How do you respect others?*

- Low Face Cultures: Direct and open communication is more important than not causing someone embarrassment or preventing conflict. Not telling the truth is less socially acceptable than getting angry with someone.

- High Face Cultures: Protecting people's honor is very important. Indirect communication is preferred and seen as more mature. Actions or words that could cause shame or embarrassment to others are to be avoided. Getting angry with others is less socially acceptable than avoiding telling the truth if doing so will hurt someone.

Saving Face

Adapted from Craig Storti, *Figuring Foreigners Out: A Practical Guide* (Yarmouth, ME: Intercultural Press, 1999), 98.

Degree of Directness

Adapted from Craig Storti, *Figuring Foreigners Out: A Practical Guide* (Yarmouth, ME: Intercultural Press, 1999), 99.

107

Locus of Control: *What change is possible?*

- Internal Locus of Control: People can control their lives and are responsible for overcoming challenges. All problems can and should be solved.

- External Locus of Control: Complex outside forces influence life and cannot be easily understood or overcome. People should accept most things in life as they can't really change them easily.

Locus of Control

Adapted from Craig Storti, *Figuring Foreigners Out: A Practical Guide* (Yarmouth, ME: Intercultural Press, 1999), 82.

Power Distance: *How do you interact with authority?*

- Low Power Distance: People under authority are free to share their ideas and speak into the decision-making process. It is possible to disagree with authority in appropriate ways. People do not like to be micromanaged.

- High Power Distance: Authority figures are expected to use their power fully for the benefit of those under their authority. People should not disagree with authority. People like to be micromanaged.

Power Distance

Adapted from Craig Storti, *Figuring Foreigners Out: A Practical Guide* (Yarmouth, ME: Intercultural Press, 1999), 140.

NOTES

Unit 1

1. Robert J. Priest, "Short-Term Missions as a New Paradigm," in *Mission After Christendom: Emergent Themes in Contemporary Mission*, ed. Ogbu U. Kalu, Peter Vethanayagamony, and Edmund Kee-Fook Chia (Louisville, KY: Westminster John Knox Press, 2010), 86.

2. Robert Wuthnow, *Boundless Faith: The Global Outreach of American Churches* (Berkeley, CA: University of California Press, 2009), 171.

3. Robert J. Priest and Joseph Paul Priest, "'They See Everything and Understand Nothing': Short-Term Mission and Service Learning," *Missiology* 36, no. 1 (January 2008): 57.

4. Wuthnow, *Boundless Faith*, 180.

5. Ibid., 180.

6. Bryant L. Myers, *Walking with the Poor: Principles and Practices of Transformational Development* (Maryknoll, NY: Orbis Books, 1999), 86.

Unit 2

1. David A. Livermore, *Serving with Eyes Wide Open: Doing Short-Term Missions with Cultural Intelligence* (Grand Rapids, MI: Baker Publishing Group, 2006), 90–91.

Unit 3

1. This is a modification of the definition of paternalism found in Roland Bunch, *Two Ears of Corn: A Guide to People-Centered Agricultural Improvement* (Oklahoma City, OK: World Neighbors, 1982), 19–23.

Unit 4

1. Livermore, *Serving with Eyes Wide Open*, 95–96.

2. "Michael" and "Shelley," interview by Katie Casselberry, March 11, 2014.

3. Marco Perez, interview by Katie Casselberry, Lookout Mountain, GA, January 15, 2013.

4. "Jason," interview by Katie Casselberry, October 30, 2013.

Unit 5

1. Miriam Adeney, "The Myth of the Blank Slate: A Check List for Short-Term Missions," in *Effective Engagement in Short-Term Missions: Doing it Right!*, ed. Robert J. Priest (Pasadena, CA: William Carey Library, 2008), 132.

Unit 6

1. We are incredibly grateful for the input of Kurt Ver Beek, Jo Ann Van Engen, and David Livermore, whose comments influenced this unit, as well as units 7 and 8.

2. The questions in this section also reflect insights from "Michael" and "Shelley," interview.

Unit 8

1. Priest and Priest, "'They See Everything and Understand Nothing,'" 57.

2. Dennis Horton, Sarah Caldwell, Rachel Calhoun, Josh Flores, Chris Gerac, and Gabrielle Leonard, "Short-Term Mission Trips: What the Long-Term Mission Personnel Really Think about Them," *The Year 2013 Annual Proceedings of the ASSR*, ed. Jon K. Loessin and Scott Stripling (2013): 71.

ACKNOWLEDGMENTS

This project is a result of the encouragement and work of countless people, including:

Katie Casselberry, who shepherded this project from start to finish, using her vast skills at research, writing, and organization. Without Katie's commitment, dedication, and perseverance, this project would never have been completed.

Andy Jones of the Chalmers Center and our team at Moody Publishers, including Duane Sherman, Pam Pugh, and Parker Hathaway, who worked tirelessly to bring this project to fruition.

David Livermore, Jo Ann Van Engen, and Kurt Ver Beek, who graciously reviewed several units of this project and shared their insights and experiences with us. Thank you for your collaboration and encouragement.

The many church and ministry leaders who shared their wisdom, perspectives, and stories with us as we crafted the written manuscript, including Ron Barnes, Gregg Burgess, David Campbell, Scott Dewey, Jeff Galley, Opal Hardgrove, Sam Haupt, Shawn Janes, Kurt Kandler, Cathi Linch, Joel and Krista McCutcheon, Sam Moore, Marco Perez, Donald Thompson, Greg and Bobbi Van Schoyck, and James Ward.

John Holberg and Callie Dixon, who contributed to the research and revision process. Thank you for being so generous with your time and gifts.

The team at RightNow Media, especially Justin Forman, Phil Warner, Mark Blitch, and Mark Weaver, who crafted the videos that accompany this project.

The 410 Bridge, Mercy Ministries, Sunshine Gospel Ministries, Videre, and the countless people who coordinated and participated in interviews for the video units: Scott and Melanie Dewey, Crizauld Francois, Jedlain Geffrard, Joel Hamernick, Kurt Kandler, Diane

Pulvermiller, James Ward, and many others.

The teams from North Point Church, 12Stone Church, and Hixson Presbyterian Church, who graciously allowed us to film their visits in Haiti and Chicago. Thanks for allowing us to join you and share your reflections.

All the pastors and church leaders we have met who are trying to mobilize their congregations to advance Christ's kingdom, including Juan Constantino, Patrick Dominguez, Steve Daugherty, Sarah Frank, Jeff Galley, Bobby Griffith, David Hardin, Scott Harris, Jeff Jernigan, Gretchen Kerr, Johnny Long, Mary McClear, Andy Merrick, Mike Miller, Maria Penzes, Jeff Redding, Tim Ritter, Ray Sanabria, Chris Seaton, Doug Serven, Jason Surratt, Mark Swarner, Marcia Trani, Lorena Valle, Scott Wiggins, Barry Wilks, and countless others.

I (Steve) was so blessed by the support of my amazing partner and wife Mary, my seven kids and two sons-in-law, my church, and my Covenant College students. They all prayed for me and encouraged me as I worked on this project and completed my teaching responsibilities.

I (Brian) want to thank my wonderful wife, Jill, and my three fantastic children for their enduring support and encouragement of my work with the Chalmers Center, including this project. As important as this work is to me, it pales in comparison to them.

As always, all praise and glory to God for His continual grace and mercy in our lives. Jesus Christ's power to make all things new, both in our lives and in the world through His church, is our only hope and salvation.

—Steve Corbett and Brian Fikkert